The Changing Seasons

Winter

Paul Humphrey

FRANKLIN WATTS
LONDON • SYDNEY

This edition 2012

Franklin Watts
338 Euston Road
London NW1 3BH

Franklin Watts Australia
Level 17/207 Kent Street
Sydney, NSW 2000

A CIP catalogue record for this book is available
from the British Library

Dewey classification number: 578.4'3

ISBN: 978 1 4451 0715 8

Planning and production by Discovery Books Limited
Editors: Paul Humphrey, Rebecca Hunter
Designer: Jemima Lumley

Photo credits: Cardiff Council (Cardiff Winter Wonderland): title page, 11;
CFW Images/Chris Fairclough: 18, 19, 24, 27; Corbis: 16; Chris Fairclough:
10, 12, 13, 28, 29; FLPA: 4, 9 (John Watkins), 15 (S & D & K Maslowski), 17 (Terry
Whittaker), 20 (Jan Vermeer/Foto Natura); Getty Images: 8 (Scott
Markewitz/Aurora); 24 (Photonica); Rebecca Hunter: 6, 7; Istockphoto.com: 14 and
front cover (Cheryl Triplett), 22 (Elena Elisseeva), 25 top (Kelly Cline), 26;
Photodisc: 21 and back cover; Photographers Direct: 23 (Oli Gardner).

Printed in UK

Franklin Watts is a division of Hachette Children's Books,
an Hachette UK company.
www.hachette.co.uk

Contents

Winter is the season that follows autumn.

Many trees have lost
all their leaves.

7

 It is often rainy
in winter.

Sometimes there
are floods.

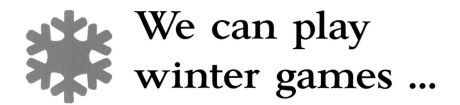

We can play
winter games ...

... or go ice skating.

It is dark and cold in the evenings.

We spend more time indoors.

13

There are lots of berries on the bushes.

Berries make good
winter food for birds.

Some animals grow a thick winter coat.

Others hibernate until
spring comes.

By the middle of winter it can get very cold with frost or snow.

It is fun to build
a snowman.

You can see animal
tracks in the snow.

These are rabbit tracks.

21

Ponds freeze up ...

... and ducks skid
on the ice.

23

We get cold when
we play outside in
the snow ...

... but we can
eat warm winter
food afterwards.

Near the end of winter, we see new lambs in the fields.

Snowdrops appear.
Spring is coming!

Winter projects

Pantomime puppets

Many people go to see a pantomime in winter. This project shows you how to make your own pantomime theatre and puppets.

You will need:

Old wooden spoons ❋ Acrylic paints ❋ Pieces of fabric and wool
Some stiff cardboard ❋ A large cardboard box ❋ Glue ❋ Sticky tape
Two large pieces of coloured crêpe paper

What to do:

1. Paint faces on the backs of the wooden spoons.
2. Cut out some body shapes from the cardboard.
3. Cut out some clothes shapes from the fabric and glue them to the body shapes.

4. Glue or tape the body shapes and clothes to the handles of the spoons.
5. Cut a large hole in the side of the cardboard box. This will be your stage.
6. Cut away the other side of the cardboard box, so that you can see all the way through.
7. Cover the rest of the box in one of the sheets of crêpe paper.
8. Use the second piece of crêpe paper to make curtains for your stage. Now you can put on a show!

Make a bird feeder

Birds often find it hard to find food in winter.
You can help them by making this easy feeder.

You will need:
An empty plastic drinks bottle ❋ Some strong string
A few wooden sticks ❋ Scissors or a sharp knife
A large bag of unsalted peanuts

What to do:
1. Ask an adult to help you cut some slits in the bottle.
2. Push the sticks through the slits so the birds will have something to perch on.
3. Cut some smaller slits so the birds can peck the nuts.

4. Fill the bottle with nuts and put the top back on.
5. Tie the string around the bottle top and hang the bottle from the branch of a tree.
6. Don't forget to fill the feeder up each day. Once the birds start using your feeder, they will come back each day for more food.
7. Record which birds visit your feeder.

29

Index